T0365329

Jeff

Appreciating OUR PETS
and Wilderness Life

Poems, Photos, and Paintings of Pets

Mary Alice Ranieri

Order this book online at www.trafford.com
or email orders@trafford.com

Most Trafford titles are also available at major online book retailers.

Print information available on the last page.

ISBN: 978-1-4907-5212-9 *(sc)*
           978-1-4907-5211-2 *(e)*

Library of Congress Control Number: 2015909019

Trafford rev. 06/27/2015

 www.trafford.com

North America & international
toll-free: 1 888 232 4444 (USA & Canada)
fax: 812 355 4082

Appreciating Our Pets
and Wilderness Life

Preface

Pets can strengthen our lives, health, and emotions. They ask only to be loved
and fed, then left alone or pampered. We have the choice.
These poems are from real events narrated by one who loves to take in all
those abused and hungry, needing a warm pad or a home-made birdhouse.

(Haiku verses are unrhymed three-lined, syllables of 5-7-5).
Rhyming couplets and lyrics comprise the remainder of
the author's creation as well as paintings, and photographs.

Curved thumb--unique type,
The hand to hold a bluebird,
To sow flower seeds.

Contents

Clarence Amos Jefferis
Pigeons are now extinct. These devoted birds served mankind well as carrier
pigeons flying messages to strategic places, even war zones, before the
advent of computers and smart phones.

The Naturalist

Orchids grow in humid holders;
Pet pigeons ride upon his shoulders
As calmly as aqua parakeets,
Unafraid of a Spaniel up-ending for treats.

Freeport swamps find Whooping Cranes,
Dipping down to beg a catch.
No longer a *secret* fishing haunt,
Clarence opens his wire-cage latch.

Pigeons feeding in a back yard haven.
1977   Allahabad, India

White-winged Dove

(pigeon family)   Mourning Dove

A turkey we named Jasper Tom escaped from a truck-load headed for the market. He was found strutting around a pond of pet ducks and geese making himself at home for about four years. . . until a hungry wolf invaded his wire fencing.

Jeff

Cameras clicked when he flared his tail--
Like opening a fan or a sail.
We wonder who opened the gate,
Allowing inside a hungry ingrate.

Toy dogs are smart
Making up for size,
So it's no surprise
They steal your heart.

Michael, shouldering Macaws and Sabina holding Austin as well. . .
From a happy island sending cards to family

Jeff

Michael pets mongrel
Gift from a nearby farmer
Background peacocks watch

Jeff

Michael goes to San Antonio
With bandit and King Ray.
The Alamo's on the way.

Painted from snapshot
Alert dog now hangs on wall
Gaffing insurance

Pigmy owl nested in my backyard hollow elm:
I waited until he left his realm
For an early morning camera shot,
Hoping he wouldn't abandon his leafy plot.

Jeff

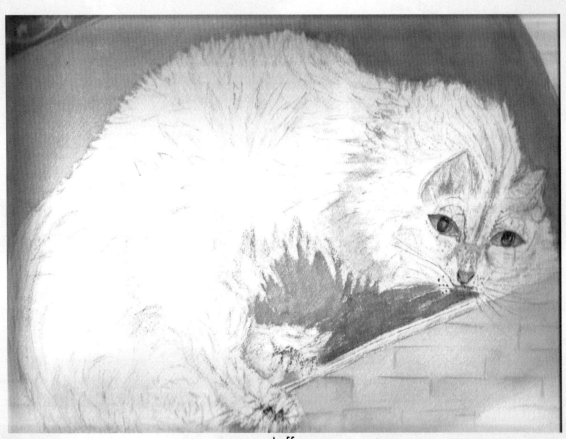

Jeff
A cat who loved the watercolor block,
Pressing the hard-pressed paper even more,
Or waiting for her turn to pose?

Near the beautiful Taj Mahal
Young sahib holds his cobra pet--
Cobra venom doth stall
Hands that reach for a   *frozen asset*.

Jeff

With feathers aglow, he steals the show
Demanding a place to strut or race,
A makeshift stage . . . Outside the cage
A place to squawk and learn to talk.

Jeff

Cockatiel clings to shoulder,
With Eddy no less bolder.

Jeff

Bantam Rooster minds the nestlings.

Mariela Campbell: remembers adoring geese as a child
in Columbia, SA. And now, though grown up,
she hugs a friend's goose, while the friend, in turn,
paints her hugging the goose.

Jeff

Choosing leadership
To fly over rural pond
Gaggling geese line-up

Home-made pond attracts
Wild geese. . . Dry dog food and corn
Attract gosling brood

Counting the hatchery

Hear my loud honking
We're set for a morning swim
Please throw out our corn

Spoonbills in flight
What an astounding sight
Domestic ducks perceived. . .
Instincts no longer retrieved/

Tina lounges on hearth
Surrounded by artifacts.
Ben Franklin stove will keep her warm
When winter chill impacts.

Freddie Jageler opts for horse back riding when
vacationing near Lake Murray, Texas.
Few horses today have to work for their masters.
They are more a pleasure to ride!

Clydesdale or Shetland Pony,
Horses saved our aching feet
Palomino or Strawberry Roan
Earned pastures green and sugar treat.

Jeff

Horses in Claremore, Oklahoma digging under snow for nutritious roots

Jeff

Pinto and Appaloosa with friends
Are grazing around the barn
Where the good grass never ends
On a well-kept farm in early morn.

Her address is 1 Box Turtle Lane. Margie Jageler, now older than snapshot, still travels frequently to other shores. Her cabbage patch doll is a pet for the very young.

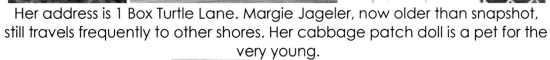

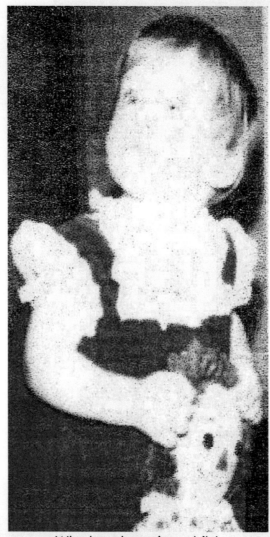

What a charming child
Jennifer clutches her doll
Her smiling rag toy

Hatched Whooping Crane
Lessens the extinction bane

Jeff

Loons cry a warning
With ducklings passing by
Floating on mama's back

Friendly Mallard watching a sleeping Muskogee:
Why can't she fly away with me?
I would enjoy her company.

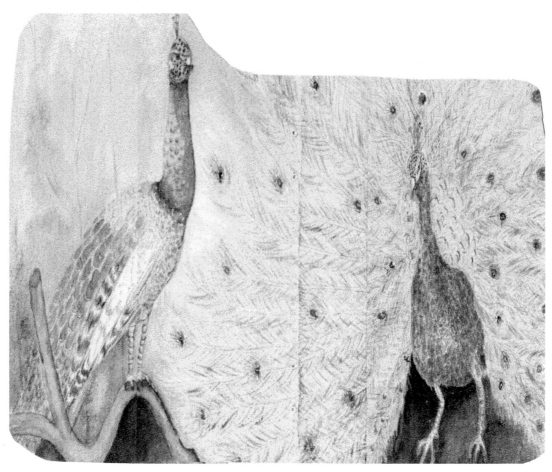

Jeff

Peahen
Peacock
A pair of beauties hatched a fledging and had to be given away due to their belligerence. No one could come within fifty feet of their young. New owners built a roomy aviary, sparing no expense for their care. Considered legally wild, they can be coaxed into becoming pets.

Parakeet Pete
Learned a few words to chirp.
When old, he fell from his perch,
Sending a message to me:
Good by Mawee!

Macaw

He peels and eats all fruit donated,
No lovlier bird hath God created!

Early springtime blooms
Hatching and pollinating
For the love of Earth

Jeff

Jeff

Sparrow shares
hamburger lunch
at roadside park.

Flamingo wader
Descending to a dark lagoon
Like a pink fairy

Bunny hides in a Jonquil bloom,
Listening for danger to loom.
He has no vocal chords for sound,
His only defense is thumping the ground.

Under spring time trees,
Over grassy leas,
The goats will pull the cart
Crafted by a loving heart.

Painted from a family album by Jeff

Indians love an elephant ride
Her pony decked for a parade
has trampted many holidays
On a lazy Sunday afternoon
and festivals.
Tourists often confide

The fear of tromping a sacred dune!

Dancing bears of New Delhi, India

Jeff

Overlooking the lake,
Watching Purple Martins build nests,
Rover lived for thirty years
Before going home to heavenly rest.

A teakwood elephant inspired the *parade* elephant painting.

Young raccoons impatient for dark
peer through the oak tree fork
wondering if the cat has left a scrap
big enough for three!

Camels explore Chinese zoo grounds.

Papa bear out of hibernation

Tina cutting teeth on her basket

Outdoors, my three Siamese
Chase cicadas in the evening breeze.
Indoors, they plan to attack
When painful ears bemoan a *vac*.

Baby parrot purchased in Ahmadabad
Knows the table will soon be filled with food.
He screeches on his favorite perch
When hunger assails his mood.

Parrots seems to mate for life,
staying impervious to strife.

Indian art: the peeple tree has a flat leaf for painting
everything from birds to Santa Claus.

Aloof, but listening, a cat pretends indifference.
Then leaps to frighten some meadow lark,
Expecting a hot pursuit.

Jeff

Kittens in verdant grass
Watching the sunset pass.

Darkness finds the Armadillo ready to dig for roots.

cats, cats, cats

just lounging between meals

I know my place!

Is the camera edible?

Listen to what the cats have to say
ESP is their language. Tune in!

Jeff

Without a sign of fear
He grazed near hill-side homes:
This tawny white-tail deer
No longer feeds nor roams.

Jeff

Deer in snow, pausing for a way to go;
Across the meadow to dig for roots.
Or follow some forsaken row
Where a farmer leaves
A few old fruits?

Mythical bird believed to recreate itself,
the Phoenix is a riot of color, as this one hanging
above the Phoenix Air Port.

Jeff

Will a barbed wire fence deter
This eight-pronged buck
Gauging the length and breadth
To spring and trust to luck?

Jeff
The buffalo may hear
Stampedes pounding hard grounds,
Ghosts of kin dodging each spear
Where their herd no longer abounds.

Crested heron stalking near our pier

Fearless stalker will angle
Fish of any length.

Joseph Ranieri

Walking through Texas Metals, I noticed the beautiful curlicues from metal cuttings and encouraged artist Joe Ranieri to transfer his talent to metal sculpturing, This life-size bull was purchased to represent the stock market's Bull Market.

Bengal tiger making colorful waves
Tiger cub chewing on bark

Ocelot *greenies*
Chewing on maple tree bark
Spawn sharp teeth. . . Strong gums

Jeff

French Poodle and Tabby share a pad
On a window seat, a favorite retreat.
They spy both feather and leaf, colorfully clad.

India's befriended civet mastered dog tricks:
Rolling over, or fetching sticks.

Jeff

Annie
Appropriate name for an orphaned cat
Befriended by squirrels; she came to my lawn,
A stranger, unafraid of a loving pat,
Now scaling my cedar house and flying down.
She'll leap on your lap
Then burrow down with a plaintive mew.

I'm not ceramic, my feathers are real
I love to be noticed with a pear to peel.

Black-bellied Whistler
No longer do I hear this tree duck
Make his special sounds--
A whistle or a cluck.

Nesting far above the ground
Migrating east to west. . .
Perhaps he's found eternal rest.

Jeff

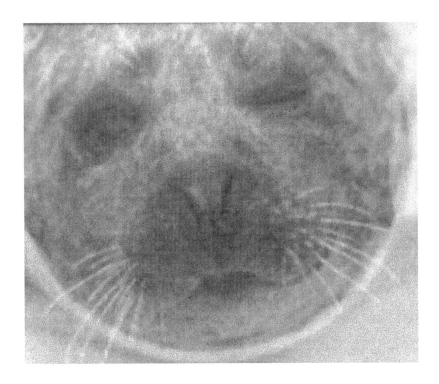

Ice forms protective shields
For hibernating seals.

Mighty winging hawk
Guided by beacon's white cloud
Predators crouch low
* * *

Jeff
Royal pair push off for a swim,
Imperial Ducks find life becoming grim:
Oil spills from tankers impede their way,
Debris from human's careless play.

A ram on the highest hill after vaulting a rill
And umpteen ledges showing off his skill.

Seeming pre-historic, some bison are still about.
Philanthropists admire their strength and clout.
Armadillos roam southwest digging triangular holes,
Nice for planting trees, a bush or flag poles.
Texas mascot: the longhorn steer--
Numbers grow fewer year by year.

Jeff

Jeff
Trumpet swans staking out a spot for nesting

RESCUERS AT WORK
VICTIMS BENEATH THE RUBBLE
CANINES SENSE FEAR.

RESCUE DOGS

On that fateful day
Hearing injured plead,
They sniffed and dug
With frantic speed.
Master's treat--his pay
Was pat on head or hug.

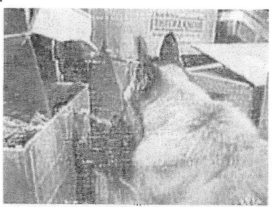

I love this old basket to recuperate from cattle dip; goodbye to vermin!

Jeff

Trailing a brother, we gather dew berries,
I grasp two mangy cats, while Joseph ferries
Across the creek on a wooden plank
To mossy ground. . .a vine-covered bank.
Then home to spare . . . a kitchen chair.

Jeff

Land of the Elk
Well-diggers and riggers bequeath pet stones.
Fossils arise from storms or quakes,
Deciduous shell and glacial crack
Exude mastodon horns. . .   and cousin-giants:
Pterodactyls, both impervious to gravitons.
We wonder what madness sealed their doom?

Flowing rivers follow the morning sun,
Dividing light and shade, Elk grazing green hills
With pecking finch. . . We grasp the tube,
The micro-chip, and bedrock amber with squiggles.

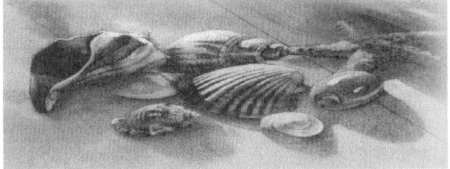

Susie found *her* pet rock at the Painted Forest

Rare white tiger sleeps
India's stone slab is *home*
Extinction begins

Rooster protectively guards our hen house entrance..
Ducklings follow mother duck:
Do they smell pond life ahead,
Or a swimming lesson to master?
Her cluck implies *there's nothing to dread*.

Silkies have feathers resembling fur
Markets find fewer hybrids to sell:
A priceless bantam whose eggs are rare
Let us incubate their precious shell!

Muskogee's find a nesting space on the ledge of the patio;
What fun to watch ducklings waddling behind moms
en route to the pond!

In one of India's many parks this red-neck crane
Strolled from table to table demanding grain,
Or any scraps of food, discarded or not,
Or else get chased out the gate of the public plot.

Red neck cranes monitor the passing parade.

Colorful birds populate   New Delhi

We named him Ralph, knowing he could not leave India.
We bid him farewell when the rickshaw pulls up to our gate
with a couple of Hindus dressed in native garb--sari and dhoti,
promising to take good care of him.

Jeff

Golden Bantam hatched
a trio with one black chick
and two butter balls

Herding cows to wind-proof barns, we shelter sheep once shorn.
Palominos graze on hay-strewn plots. Beggars limp to camper cots.
Cargi peers out his keep checking unwary sheep.

Fritter wings unfold
Flying south to warmer climes
To Old Mexico

Painting fragile butterflies
Bewitches the artist's eyes:
Burnt umber shines on wings,
Vermilion designs their rings.

The honey bee less seen today
To stage his dance for workers to follow.
his nectar blooms are miles away
Beyond flower fields now fallow.

Marching orbs impose universal will
striking a note of birth unless we march
along with our guardian soul
and the animal spirit who watches over us.

Goats eat anything, even chicken feed.

Oranges are harvested, but his dog is expecting
a different treat!

Nudging to be petted. He gets his wish.

One chilly morning
Mongrel watches me shiver
While Eddy shutters

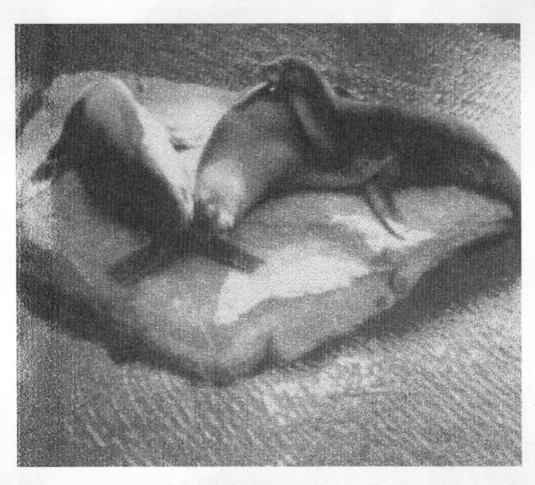

Seals in silver cay
California's Morro Bay
Amphibians play

Author's Page

My thanks to all who allowed snapshots of pets or rock collections,   Freddie and Margie Jageler, their son Michael, and to Eddy Jefferis,   Susan Ranieri, Du Bose Insurance

The zoo is world-wide--a way to observe almost all animals.
This one in Tsangchow, China had many species of chirping birds
and monkeys running outside the cage.